T0001640

A REGENCY GUIDE
to
MODERN LIFE

Editor Florence Ward
Designer Isabelle Merry
Senior Production Editor Siu Yin Chan
Senior Production Controller Louise Minihane
Managing Editor Pete Jorgensen
Managing Art Editor Jo Connor
Publishing Director Mark Searle

Written by Carly Lane
Cover and interior illustrations Jo Podmore

DK would like to thank Beth Davies for the concept, Claire Rogers for copyediting,
Madeleine Pollard for proofreading and Emma Caddy for indexing.

First American Edition, 2023
Published in the United States by
DK Publishing
1745 Broadway, 20th Floor,
New York, NY 10019

A catalog record for this book
is available from the Library of Congress.
ISBN 978-0-7440-6949-5

Copyright © 2023 Dorling Kindersley
Limited
DK, a Division of Penguin Random House
LLC
23 24 25 26 27 10 9 8 7 6 5 4 3 2 1
001-333026-Feb/2023

DK books are available at special discounts
when purchased in bulk for sales promotions,
premiums, fund-raising, or educational use.
For details, contact:
DK Publishing Special Markets,
1745 Broadway, 20th Floor,
New York, NY 10019
SpecialSales@dk.com

Printed and bound in China

For the curious
www.dk.com

All rights reserved.
Without limiting the rights under the
copyright reserved above, no part of this
publication may be reproduced, stored in
or introduced into a retrieval system, or
transmitted, in any form, or by any means
(electronic, mechanical, photocopying,
recording, or otherwise), without the prior
written permission of the copyright owner.
Published in Great Britain by Dorling
Kindersley Limited

MIX
Paper | Supporting
responsible forestry
FSC™ C018179

This book was made with Forest
Stewardship Council ™ certified
paper – one small step in DK's
commitment to a sustainable future.
**For more information go to
www.dk.com/our-green-pledge**

A REGENCY GUIDE
to
MODERN LIFE

Written by Carly Lane

Illustrated by Jo Podmore

CONTENTS

Dearest modern reader—

You may be wondering what this book has in store for you. Allow me to introduce myself. Many already know me as a lady of the *ton*, a veritable presence among the most important people to know in society, and one who never refrains from voicing her opinion on every matter under the sun. But we will dispense with unnecessary and rather lengthy titles for now; those who seek my advice are welcome to call me, quite simply, "Lady A."

Indeed, I bestow advice, giving counsel on just about every problem that can arise in life. But it is this lady's understanding that the world has changed... rather significantly, and the troubles that once weighed on many a member within my social circles are not the same ones experienced by contemporaries today. However, some issues are consistently omnipresent! The solutions for how to fix them may look rather different to how they did in my day, but on the other hand, it is a truth universally acknowledged that an individual in possession of a persistent dilemma must be in want of a lady's instruction.

Consider this your essential, illustrative (and helpfully illustrated!) Regency-era guide to your present-day struggles, whether they be rooted in romance, familial ties, platonic relationships, occupational strife, and so on. It will enable you to regard the world with a new perspective, shaped by my helpfully guiding hand. By the time you reach the very last page of this book, you will undoubtedly be able to render yourself a verifiable diamond, one that everyone else will either want to be or desire to get to know.

Yours in eternal instruction,

Lady A

CHAPTER ONE
LOVE

Whether you are experiencing the new
flowering of infatuation or the time-tested
endurance of commitment, romance in all its
stages can be quite wonderful to behold. But,
to paraphrase a great wordsmith, the course of true
love never does run smoothly, and that is where a
helpful bit of advice can go a long way.

From navigating the signals that a promising
paramour may be sending you, to deciding what
course of action to take when an attachment
has grown sour, here is my guidance for
all matters of the heart.

DECIDING WHAT YOU WANT FROM LOVE

Dear Lady A: I haven't had a serious relationship before, but I'm trying to wade into the dating pool. How do I figure out what I'm looking for in a potential partner?

Back in my day, all one had to do was sit back and rely on their ambitious matchmaking mama to arrange something for them, but nowadays things are a little more hands on! Of course, when it comes to a potential partnership, knowing exactly what you're looking for can be a bit more complicated, but this is an instance in which indecision is understandable.

Use this time for contemplation. Give yourself ample opportunity to mull over the ideal traits you want in a significant other. Do they have a delightful sense of humour? Are they capable of engaging you in witty repartee? Is compassion for others one of their strongest instincts?

Arrange a series of meetings with those who show potential and discover what fate may have in store. But do not fret, dear reader, if romance does not reveal itself immediately. In the meantime, indulge the possibility of enjoying yourself, so long as you are being transparent with your feelings!

THE WORLD OF DATING APPS

Dear Lady A: I've just moved to a new city and want to try out the dating scene. How do I navigate the world of dating apps?

This is the first time this lady has been alerted to the existence of these... *courtship applications*, but they sound marvellously economical! Combing through a cluster of potential suitors with nothing more than the swipe of a finger is certainly an improvement over having to wait for the next society ball to meet the eligible matches available that season.

It may seem a bit daunting, but the fact that prospective partners are required to fill out a questionnaire about themselves should make your pursuit of romance more convenient. You can dismiss those with whom you will likely have little in common based on their responses, while matching with ones who share your particular interests. Even if it doesn't amount to romance, there is also the possibility of making new friends in the process. This author sees no reason not to make your presence known for the sheer opportunities right under your fingertips. After all, nothing ventured, nothing gained!

DOROTHEA, 25
3 MILES AWAY

5'6, LOVE WALTZING +
FENCING, OFTEN FOUND
WITH A GLASS OF CLARET.
LOOKING FOR SOMEONE
TO PROMENADE WITH ;)

GOING ON A FIRST DATE

*Dear Lady A: I'm about to go on a first date with someone
I really like. How do I make it a special experience
—and guarantee that there will be more dates?*

Is there anything more thrilling than the prospect of
romance blossoming on the horizon? I dare say there's
not a feeling in the world that can replicate the excitement
of the beginnings of a courtship. Gone are the days in which
a gentleman might call upon you at your home and wait to
be shown into the sitting room by your footman. Apparently,
these days a potential suitor does not even need to seek
permission from your parents to request the pleasure of
your company on an afternoon drive or a stroll in the park.
You are afforded every possible independence and privilege
to accept such invitations on your own behalf.

First, this author suggests that if you allow your suitor to
decide the sequence of events on this particular outing,
you should be willing to experience the thrill of surprise!
You may be introduced to a new activity that you have
never pursued before, which promises an exciting possibility
of romance.

After all, permitting your paramour to guide you in something new is not only a way to foster trust, but also something that can encourage a team effort. There may be no better barometer of compatibility than discovering firsthand how well you two can work together! Furthermore, do not underestimate the importance of chatting up one another. It is crucial that you not only take the time to learn about your paramour's interests, but also have the chance to communicate your own. Conversing over an intimate dinner is an exceedingly romantic way to strike the right mood—and who does not look their best when illuminated by candlelight?

CATCHING FEELINGS

Dear Lady A: I've been casually seeing someone, but I'm actually starting to fall for them. How do I deal with these unexpected feels?

There is something quite daring when it comes to pursuing an informal affair—if the most notorious rakes can do so, why can't the rest of us engage in such things from time to time? Perhaps the two of you have been waltzing together at more than one ball, which would certainly set tongues wagging. Or perhaps you have been promenading with them through the park several times in the same week.

You may not be able to ascertain whether this person is ready to make a greater commitment to you without professing the truth of your feelings—and this can and often does require a great deal of courage. The alternative, however, would involve you remaining trapped in a vicious cycle, uncertain of whether or not your deeper affections are reciprocated. It is far better to make your "feels" known to this person through honesty rather than lingering in a state of torment.

CAUGHT IN A LOVE TRIANGLE

Dear Lady A: I'm stuck in an impossible situation!
I think I might have feelings for more than one person
at the same time. What do I do?

The nature of the heart can be a perplexing one, can it not, especially when one might have romantic inclinations for not just one person, but two? This writer does not envy you your position, as these matters can become very entangled and very complicated if you do not take steps to be open and honest about what you are feeling, ideally as quickly as possible. After all, you may have more than one heart hanging in the balance—including your own.

That is not to say that you should not tread with caution in your honesty; some hearts might be bruised regardless of how mindfully you act. Such things should be handled with a particular amount of delicacy and care, so the best course of action is to simply take aside each prospective person and explain the truth of your most ardent feelings—perhaps underneath an open gazebo, or in a misty field while the sun rises over the hill. That is a foolproof means of learning whether or not your affections are reciprocated.

BEING GHOSTED

WUU2?

Dear Lady A: Someone I've been seeing has stopped responding to my messages. The last time I reached out, they left my texts on read. I think I've been ghosted! What do I do?

Darling reader, do you mean to tell me that you are, at this present moment, being haunted by some sort of spectre? That your former paramour has, in fact, ceased to be upon this mortal coil and sloughed off the shackles of existence? This is the stuff that Gothic novels are made of!

If, however, you are actually referring to the notion of your sweetheart performing a very regrettable disappearance, then you have my utmost sympathies. This is not something that anyone, most importantly you, deserves to encounter. In fact, that they would be willing to sever ties so unexpectedly says more about them than you. You could make an effort to reconnect with them at the earliest convenience, but this may not necessarily correct the larger problem long-term. If they remain strangely absent in your life, this lady suggests that you move on without a backward glance, and try not to take it too deeply to heart.

LIVING WITH YOUR PARTNER

Dear Lady A: My partner and I recently decided to move in together, but I'm worried their personal habits will clash with mine. How do we find a compromise?

My dear, the solution to your dilemma is right there in your very question: compromise! The decision to share a domicile is an exciting one, but it certainly will not be without some sort of adjustment period for you both. Perhaps your beloved has always been more of an early riser, while you are more likely to stay awake into the young hours, letting the wick burn low as you read. (As an aside, this lady would not recommend doing anything that would cause your eyes significant strain, given that squinting can be very unbecoming.)

Not addressing your differences could lead to some ill will between you in future, so it is imperative that you establish an open channel of communication from the start. Clearly outline your preferences and where they might diverge. Then again, it is not so important for you to always be together either. If your paramour wants to greet the day early while you lie abed a while longer, where is the harm in that?

A certain level of personal space is indeed healthy and necessary for any relationship to flourish!

The notion of introducing another person into that setting could prove jarring at first. But take me at my word: it will not always be so. Change is not always a disruption, and in many instances it is the very thing that keeps us from becoming too set in our ways, too stagnant and unwilling to evolve. Regard this as the true opportunity that it is—for you and your partner to challenge one another's conventions but ultimately bring out the very best in one another along the way.

MEETING THE PARENTS

Dear Lady A: I'm meeting my partner's family for the first time this weekend. How can I ensure that I make the best impression on them?

Let me provide initial reassurance, gentle advice-seeker: you are in this situation because your betrothed holds you in high regard. Why would they introduce you to their family if they did not consider you someone who is worthy of admiration? Keep that in mind as you begin your preparations to meet the people who could very well become your future in-laws, and do not forget to hold your head high, as good posture can lead to a very strong first impression.

You should present yourself properly upon first being welcomed into their abode. In other words, do not forget to bow or curtsy. You can also elect towards a simple handshake, as is apparently more appropriate for this modern age. Tradition also dictates that callers should not impose upon the host for a long time, so trust that the visit will be over sooner than you know it, and you can release the breath you have undoubtedly been holding in.

KNOWING WHEN TO BREAK UP

*Dear Lady A: My partner and I have been drifting apart for a
while, and I think it's time for us to go our separate ways.
How do I break things off?*

Whatever your feelings at this moment in time, the
truth remains that it is never an easy task to dissolve
a love affair. The two of you might simply be in very different
stages of your lives than when you first embarked on this
liaison, or your affection for one another may have begun
to wane. Trust your instincts; if you are beginning to feel
doubts about the future, there could be a very reasonable
explanation for it. Simultaneously, you should take care not
to act rashly; be sure to devote serious thought to the matter.

Take an approach that is born from honesty as well as respect
when it comes to your soon-to-be former paramour. It may
lessen the sting of separation somewhat if you approach the
inevitable conversation with care—though there will likely
be tears nonetheless.

You are the best judge of your own happiness, and if you
decide that going it on your own restores that contentment,
that is a brave decision indeed.

STAYING FRIENDS
WITH AN EX

*Dear Lady A: Recently, my ex and I broke up
and it was hard on us both. Is there any way for us to
stay friends after this?*

While many of the dilemmas that you could present to this writer would guarantee an easy answer—which spoon is most appropriate for eating soup, for instance, or what the use of a fan can signal to your dancepartner—this situation does not lend itself to a definitive response.

There are some who can remain on perfectly friendly terms with their old flames, and continue that acquaintance even as each party moves on to a new attachment. There are other parties who find maintaining a connection with a former lover quite painful—and both responses are valid.

You may be feeling very tender in the aftermath of a break up, and for that reason, you would benefit from asserting personal space for a while—at least until you feel more clear-headed about your future. If your aim is to pursue a friendship, do not be afraid to assert some distance for yourself first until you can verify where your heart—and head—truly lies.

DEALING WITH HEARTBREAK

Dear Lady A: My partner and I just broke up.
It was a mutual decision, but I still feel terrible about it.
How do I get past it?

My dearest reader, there may be no pain as acute or as devastating as that of a broken heart. You have my utmost sympathies as you grieve the ending of this relationship—for it is certainly worth lamenting the choice to part ways as you would any loss in life, even if was the most mutually beneficial decision for you both.

There is no widely accepted means by which to mourn the end of a liaison. But you are certainly not expected to simply smile and bear it, let alone immediately wade back into the social pool of eligible bachelors or bachelorettes. With that in mind, what is most proper and good at this moment is for you to take care of yourself. Indulge the need to cry when you must, and permit yourself to enjoy a box of chocolates or a bowl of decadent ice cream (one hears that it can cure just about every poor mood). In time, your heart will heal, and perhaps then you may even be ready for the possibility of new romance.

LONG-DISTANCE RELATIONSHIPS

Dear Lady A: My partner and I have been in a long-distance relationship for several months now. How can I keep the romance feeling fresh and exciting while we're apart?

There is one activity I cannot recommend highly enough as you and your beloved endure a period of separation: correspondence, and at regular intervals! Handwritten letters are not only the perfect means of expressing how you feel, but you may also add personalized touches—like a spritz of perfume or cologne, or perhaps even a lock of hair so that they may keep a piece of you close until you are no longer parted by distance.

Of course, in today's day and age, it has come to this author's attention that you can also communicate through a method known as texting, the etiquette of which lies outside the realm of total comprehension. But when distilled down to its simplest qualities, a message is still a message, is it not? Although such means can be considered impersonal, the road to success is built upon small but meaningful communiques that can return affection with sincere and equal regard.

You should make use of several different approaches when sending word to your paramour. Expand upon your admiration for them at length in electronic letters. Purchase or craft for them the occasional surprise gift—even a small one will do! Send them photographs of things you've spotted in the world around you that bring fond memories of them to mind. Speak to them directly whenever possible so that you may hear the sound of each other's voices and know that your devotion remains strong. And, most importantly, remember that you will someday be in their presence again. Absence normally has one effect on the heart, after all.

ENJOYING SINGLEDOM

Dear Lady A: These days, it feels like all of my friends are in relationships and I'm still single. How do I enjoy being the one who's flying solo?

It can be difficult, yes, when you feel as though you are on an island all to yourself—or perhaps that you might be consigned to a lifetime of solitude when all of your dearest friends are finding partners. Indeed, in those times it can be nearly impossible not to compare your contentment to theirs and believe that they are happier simply because they have formed attachments—but this is a misperception.

What you need to remember chiefly, dear advice-seeker, is that you possess an inherent freedom solely based on the fact that you are, for the present moment, on your own. You have independence, and do not need to seek or consider another's opinion on the choices you make. There is something rather wonderful about that, is there not?

But take heart, for there is also every possibility that the right dashing or lovely stranger will find their way into your life when you least expect them to.

WHEN TO SAY "I LOVE YOU"

♥ ♥
♥

*Dear Lady A: My partner and I have been dating for
a while, and I think I'm finally ready to tell them I love them.
When should I take the plunge?*

Hearty salutations to you on the success of your love affair! It isn't every day that infatuation blossoms into true and unceasing affection, so you should welcome it with open arms when it does.

That said, actually professing said love can feel akin to standing on the edge of a precipice, looking out into the abyss of a great unknown! It is exhilarating and terrifying in equal measure, but that is all the more reason for you to summon courage into every bone in your body and openly and unmistakably profess your ardour. For all you know, your most esteemed partner could also have been weighing up whether to express their own feelings for some time.

There is nothing more important in this world than informing those you love that you do love them, especially when life is so often unpredictable. Don't be afraid to express your feelings, for you may regret it if you don't.

CHAPTER TWO
FRIENDS

For all of the value that material possessions may hold, there may be nothing so needed in life as the friends one makes. Our friendships not only offer us comfort and solace in difficult times, but encourage us when we are in need of an extra bit of confidence — and make life brighter on the whole!

Are you having a tricky time with your friendships and are at a loss as to what to do? Do you find yourself struggling with how to forge new ones? There is no need to fret, darling reader. Read on for my indispensable advice on how to not only make friends — but keep them.

MAKING
NEW FRIENDS

*Dear Lady A: I've just moved to a new city and I don't
know the first thing about trying to meet new people.
How do I join a friend group?*

The fact that you are being so carefully discerning about
this very dilemma is proof that you are exactly the type
of person that is worth befriending! Between you and me,
there are some individuals here in the *ton* that do not concern
themselves with being amiable to the concept of friendship —
and that makes them rather insufferable, indeed.

It can be very difficult to establish one's circle of confidants
when you are in a new place, but what you might try to
ascertain is whether there are any social groups dedicated to
activities of shared interest. Perhaps you are skilled at the
pianoforte, or you would like to discuss the latest (and
somewhat scandalous) novel making the rounds in society.
This lady has heard of groups being formed on Facebook,
Instagram and other online platforms, and while I have not
ventured into such a realm myself, word is that these are
wonderful places to meet like-minded individuals and arrange
a rendezvous face-to-face. Make your presence known there,
and see what potential friendships arise!

FAIRWEATHER
FRIENDS

Dear Lady A: One of my friends seems to only appear when they need something from me. Should I keep trying to maintain this relationship, or finally let it go?

Few things are as valuable as a solid friendship, but even that is only worth its weight in gold when both parties put effort into prioritizing it. If you are not feeling propped up by a confidant, and often find yourself tasked in the role of emotionally stabilizing their needs without reciprocation, then that is an unbalanced relationship indeed.

The first port of call is to raise the issue with your friend personally. Strive to approach with kindness, especially if you are interested in preserving your camaraderie. Tell them that, while you have made yourself present for their strife, you have felt quite overlooked in comparison. It could be that your friend isn't aware of their oversight. Perhaps their neglect has been the inadvertent cause of personal troubles they are facing. However, if they do offer an indication that they are not likely to improve any time soon, this may be the signal you require to let the friendship dissolve naturally.

WHEN YOUR COUPLED FRIENDS BREAK UP

Dear Lady A: Two of my friends, who have been in a relationship for years, have just broken up. Is it possible for me to stay friends with both of them?

Dear reader, I have personal experience with this very dilemma, as one of my closest bosom friends, Lady Violet, found herself on the receiving end of a broken engagement with the Earl of Wessex, another fond companion. I was caught betwixt them, subject to their frequent inquiries about one another. (If you ask me, that indicates the possibility of their reconciliation!) These days, one can dissolve a betrothal with little to no fanfare, but that does not always ring true for the broken hearts in the wake of the break up.

In your instance, the best thing you can do is to be present for each of your friends individually, especially if you have equal bonds with them. Be there to extend your consolations, whether through unspoken assistance or by taking each on a fun outing, but try to steer clear of indulging one in any gossip about the other. Perhaps in time, you will all be able to amicably coexist.

OVERLY COMPETITIVE FRIENDS

Dear Lady A: One of my friends always gets so competitive on game night that many of us don't really want to play with them anymore. How should we broach the subject?

A bit of competition is natural—and healthy, in several cases—but it sounds as though things are no longer fun and games for your circle of friends, doesn't it? One person's tendency to venture too far into contentious territory in an otherwise amiable match of pall-mall or a few rounds of whist can sour the mood for the remainder of the group! Not only that, but it seems that the possibility of more games in the future with said friend has been thrown into question.

Bear in mind that the situation may be more subconscious than nefarious. Your friend may act in this manner because they feel that they have something to prove; or they could simply have an overly competitive nature.

Chances are they do not even realize their behavior is casting a gloom over your games. Kindly bring it to their attention, and if things do not improve, you can always suggest alternative activities for your parties that will leave everyone in greater spirits.

WHEN A FRIEND BREAKS A PROMISE

*Dear Lady A: Recently, a friend of mine made a promise
to me that they broke. They don't even seem that sorry.
How should I handle it?*

It is difficult, in these instances, not to feel as though one
has been betrayed, even to the smallest extent, and it would
never be my wish to discount your feelings as anything but
valid. However, it is never wise to assume that someone you
are close to has acted out of a particular malice or with intent
to do you harm. Perhaps your friend did not mean to
transgress, and now that they have, they are too embarrassed
to approach you and apologize, even though the gesture
would be meaningful to you.

What this may call for, dearest reader, is for you to take
initiative and extend the olive branch. Invite your friend to
call on you at home and set out an inviting spread with tea.
This will assist in setting a mood of understanding rather than
one that could provoke defensiveness. Then, gently enquire
about why they may have acted as they did, and inform them
of how hurtful it was. Give them a chance to explain their
actions to you personally, so that nothing is further
miscommunicated.

LIVING WITH A MESSY FLATMATE

Dear Lady A: I recently moved into an apartment with a friend. It's only been a few weeks, but our personal habits have started to grate on each other's nerves. How can I cope?

It can be difficult to determine exactly how two people will endure one another until they are inhabiting the same living quarters, whether by choice or by requirement. It can be more distressing when one discovers that another's habits are in direct opposition to one's own. One of you may be the more fastidious sort when it comes to performing various chores around the home, such as sweeping the floors or tending to the fireplace, while the other is content to neglect it until distressing levels of dust form. Perhaps one is not inclined to wash out the best porcelain tea set after personal use and simply leave it to soak with the rest of the dishes, while the other will track in mud from the soles of their riding boots without thought!

Remember this, though: you would not have agreed to dwell with your friend if the thought of doing so had not appealed to you—at least, initially. You may have recognized something in their preferences that would serve to complement your own. Are there duties in particular that you enjoy carrying out yourself? Perhaps you're fond of folding the laundry, and they're more content with washing the dishes. Or you would rather be the one taking on the role of head chef in the kitchen while they wield a duster on the shelves. You must consider this an opportunity to collaborate in favor of one another's strengths rather than simply making note of areas in which you find fault. In this, you can effectively remind yourself of the reasons you held for wanting to coexist in the first place—and make memories based on cooperation instead of conflict.

THAT FOMO FEELING

Dear Lady A: I'm an introvert, but when I need a break from socializing, I feel like I'm missing out on my friends' fun. How do I deal with these feelings when they come to a head?

The fact remains, my good letter-writer, that it is simply impossible for anyone to respond to every single invitation that lands on their doorstep. Why, my dearest darling friend the Marchioness of Midvale has the busiest social calendar of anyone in the *ton*, and even she does not attend all of the balls she is invited to week after week. While it is important to maintain a firm standing in your social circle, your health (of body and mind) is more significant and valuable. There are means by which you can lessen your fears of missing out on all of the fun, however, and it turns out they are very easy to achieve.

First and foremost, you must remember that outward appearances can be deceiving. What can resemble a thrilling society event could actually be closer to an excruciating ordeal. One of your friends might be subjected to the most boring conversation with a particularly loquacious earl who boasts of many personal achievements. Another could be forced to endure the clumsy footsteps of a dance partner. Yet another might be having a secretly dismal night for reasons that have little to do with the party and more with their own private business. The common denominator here is that any images that might be captured and then displayed externally to the rest of the world are chosen to make the subjects look their best, and may not be an accurate representation of what is truly occurring behind the scenes. Ultimately, my dear, these missing-out feelings will subside, and the next time you are in your friends' company, they will be all the more ecstatic to see you.

ENVYING A FRIEND'S SUCCESS

Dear Lady A: Lately, one of my friends has been very successful professionally, and it makes me feel like I haven't done much by comparison. What do I do about this unwelcome envy?

The green-eyed monster within us can be a very pervasive creature, prone to awakening at the most inopportune times. Everyone, no matter their achievements in life, will have experienced this feeling. There is every likelihood that your compatriot has undoubtedly harboured their own enviousness at times!

Your friend may be benefitting from a trough of accomplishments at the moment, but that does not mean you won't experience any fulfilment of your own when the time comes. For now, do not fret about measuring yourself against your perception of success. Consider this as well: would you not want your friend to be happy for you whenever you reach a desired milestone in your life? The most important emotion you can adopt in moments like these is not regret about what you may not have achieved, but joy on their behalf. This sentiment will bring the two of you much closer together, as you share in celebrating one another's victories.

GROWING APART FROM A FRIEND

Dear Lady A: I'm worried my bestie and I are growing out of our friendship. Our interests have changed and so have our friends. How do I hold on to this connection?

entle reader, this may be one of the few instances in which you will not like the advice that I have to impart—but there are some relationships, however precious they may be to you, that have run their course and reached their fullest potential. This hardly means that you have been found wanting, or that this is a sign of some personal failing. It is simply that the companionship you have kept close to your heart for many years has accomplished all that it was meant to from the start, and now the two of you are in significantly different places than you were when you first set out on this journey together. You are certainly not the young person you were five or ten years ago; you have experienced many more of life's tribulations since then, and it is only natural that the presence of those around you changes as you do. When these shifts occur, you will have the opportunity to make new friendships that possess their own meaning, without detracting from the importance of the relationships you have kept in the past.

That said, you may be able to maintain this current friendship if both of you are committed to regular engagements with one another—perhaps you might call on them at home, or the two of you could have a standing appointment for tea during which you can catch up on your lives. These are perfectly acceptable ways through which you can ensure that your close association continues. Provided that your most devoted friend is also willing to meet you wherever you are in your life now, you can avoid letting the ties between you fray.

KEEPING A SECRET

Dear Lady A: My friend recently told me something in confidence, but I'm also known for being a blabbermouth. How can I keep their secret and their trust without spilling all the deets?

If there is one thing I know—and I am confident in my knowledge of quite a lot—it is that secrets have a way of unearthing themselves, and always within clear hearing of the most gossipy members of the *ton*. However, we do not need to be responsible for helping them along, do we? The very fact remains that your friend's secret is just that: theirs. This means it is no one else's to divulge, declare, or so much as hint at in conversation. Now, if your reputation as a scandalmonger precedes you, this means that there is every chance others will seek you out for the slightest whiff of a new development in your companion's affairs. So I will attempt to arm you against this eventuality.

The recommendation I offer is that you should refrain from letting the conversation come around to the subject of your friend to begin with, as this would be a surefire way to see your tongue loosened and your worst tendencies come to light. Should someone in your circle attempt to bring them up in even the subtlest manner, simply respond that you are not comfortable with pursuing the topic at hand and suggest an alternative. Bring every party's attention to the latest dress in the modiste's front window, or regale them with the with thrillingly lurid details from the novel you're currently reading. If you find yourself continually pressed after trying to divert to a different subject, you may have to make your excuses and depart the discussion entirely. Your friend has bestowed their secret on you as sign of utmost trust, and in turn, keeping it is a sign of the respect you have for your friend. What's more, they clearly believe in your ability to remain loyal!

LISTENING TO A FRIEND'S DILEMMA

Dear Lady A: I'm not the best listener, but I want to work on it for my friend's sake. How can I keep myself from zoning out while my BFF is venting?

This author certainly understands the tendency to want to daydream, especially if one's mind is already prone to wandering. I think back to the latest society ball where I "zoned out," as you say, while in the midst of speaking with a very monotonous marquess twice my age! Truth be told, I am convinced that he simply wanted to hear himself talk more than he cared about anything I had to say.

This, however, is not a tedious man enjoys the sound of his own voice. This is presumably a dear friend, so it is important to prevent yourself from becoming distracted at the first opportunity. Consider how you would prefer to be engaged with. Listen appropriately, posing questions at natural intervals in the conversation. If your friend is divulging something that has been weighing on their conscience, inquire about how best you can lend your support. Perhaps they only require the one thing you are capable of providing: an open ear.

CHAPTER THREE
FAMILY

Family can lend itself to a great many dilemmas. There is lineage, of course, and the potential of a title that may be passed on to you. But there are also matters of strengthening bonds with siblings, proving yourself to parents, or creating a family of your own that exists without any direct blood relation whatsoever.

A family can take many different shapes and sizes— and there are many ways for one to survive their family, even with all of its potential complications. Continue reading for my dispensation of useful suggestions.

ASSERTING YOURSELF TO YOUR PARENTS

Dear Lady A: My parents have always been overly critical of my decision-making, especially now that I'm an adult. How do I convince them to take me seriously or respect my choices?

I t is a truth universally acknowledged that mothers and fathers are wont to believe their children are always seeking advice or input on various life matters—when often they are not! This writer knows of several meddling mamas who cannot help but become involved in furthering what they believe is their child's utmost potential. Of course, they likely will have hardly paused to consult their child's feelings in the process.

The answer for you is to approach any conversation you have with your parents in a calm manner. If you enter in a state of heightened feeling, that will only dictate the tenor of the exchange. Whatever choice you are making, whether a big occupational decision or a simpler dilemma of what to wear, gently explain your position and give your parents time to respond. You may be surprised by their willingness to finally acknowledge you with the respect to which you're entitled. Broaching these talks is never easy, but a cool head will ultimately prevail.

SIBLING RIVALRIES

Dear Lady A: Ever since we were kids, my siblings and I have always got on each other's nerves. Now that we're adults, how do we stop pushing each other's buttons?

As someone in possession of a fair number of siblings myself, courtesy of my parents' efforts to ensure the legacy of their estate could pass to at least one viable heir, you have my utmost commiseration. However, consider the alternative — that one could instead be entirely alone without brothers or sisters to rely on at all! Those of us with kin of this nature have a tendency to take them for granted more than we ought, simply because we have grown up with them for a long time and couldn't possibly fathom the alternative.

But I would beseech you to remember that your siblings may not always be this close, whether in proximity or in affection. I think of my younger sister Kitty, who was sent away and installed as a companion to our wealthy Great-Aunt Hortensia. Had I known we would be parted, and that she would forever be consigned to playing whist with geriatric members of the aristocracy, I would have treasured the moments we spent together more significantly. In your particular instance, permit me to bestow some advice: the next time you feel that one of your siblings is causing your anger to brew, inform them of exactly what you have written to me about. Tell them you wish to stop prodding at each other, in spite of what history might dictate, and instead prioritize the forging of new, positive memories. This way, you will have fonder things to look back on, rather than the regret of letting an improved dynamic slip through your fingers. Let my past be a lesson to your hopeful future!

DEALING WITH PARENTAL PRESSURE

Dear Lady A: I'm looking at universities to apply to, but my parents have strong opinions on where I should go. How do I tell them I can't cope under this type of pressure?

Given that you are already on the cusp of such a significant life change, not to mention the pressure that comes with submitting yourself for consideration to these academies, it is understandable that you do not want this additional weight of expectation on your shoulders. Alas, many parents are not always cognizant of the fact that their hopes and dreams are not shared by their children, nor are they aware that their insistence on such dreams can border on the intolerable.

Your parents' wishes stem from a place of love; they want you to be fulfilled and content in life, but because your choices look different from what they have envisioned, they may not realize that you are seeking the exact same thing. If you have already taken the time to thoroughly research and consider your course of action, now you must demonstrate to them the benefits of your decision! They will not know unless you inform them personally.

ENDURING FAMILY REUNIONS

Dear Lady A: My parents have invited me to theirs for the holidays, with some extended family I don't see eye-to-eye with. How can I survive the visit?

Ah yes, the dreaded family reunion. There are, of course, significantly more pleasant invitations that one could receive, but I'm afraid that every once in a while, we must face events that we are not entirely looking forward to. Thankfully, there are many ways in which you can not only survive but thrive. It all entails finding small but opportune means of entertaining yourself, unless you can rely on others to supply that for you with their antics.

Steering the conversation onto topics that interest you can be a way of making it more enjoyable (even if certain family members believe that their opinion on anything under the sun supplants yours). If the conversation becomes truly intolerable, try excusing yourself for a necessary refreshment (a convenient reason to exit the room without them being any the wiser). Alternatively, slip a small tome into your reticule, in case you can flee to the nearest library or study for a bit of escapism.

Be sure not to linger too long, however, as someone particularly nosy might start to outwardly enquire about your location. As long as you continue to reappear at regular intervals, that may be sufficient enough not to arouse any suspicion in curious family members. Barring all of that, you could even simply feign illness or exhaustion and proclaim that you must retire to bed early. An utterly foolproof method. Besides, there is no bad mood—even one brought on by a difficult family—that cannot be improved by a good night of sleep.

LIVING WITH YOUR PARENTS

Dear Lady A: Since I lost my job and moved in with my parents, it's been a nightmare. How do I get them to respect me as another adult under the same roof?

This author understands your predicament quite well. There are those in society who have yet to marry and, as a result, are resigned to inhabiting the same space as their parents until they make an auspicious match. Think of the ladies who made their debuts several seasons ago and still have not secured a proposal, or the second son who does not yet have to settle down solely because he is not the heir to his family's estate! There is freedom in being able to make one's own choices, especially when it pertains to one's future. But what happens when one feels trapped due to events beyond their control? Many of us have found ourselves in the same situation, of that I can assure you. But there's no reason to convince yourself it will be forever! This too will pass.

In some ways, your parents may always view you as a child, especially since they hold memories of you at a tender and reliant age. So do take care to offer them some patience. However, they should also be willing to acknowledge you as a grown individual who has thrived on your own strengths. The quickest way to assert this realization in their minds is for you to demonstrate that you are responsible and determined to restore yourself to independence as quickly as possible, such as by searching for a new form of employment. It will be impossible for them to dismiss visible evidence of your maturity if you display it to them! However, it may behove both you and your parents to operate under a landlord-tenant relationship in the meantime, with you financially contributing wherever possible, and offering to prepare meals. A dynamic consisting of mutual support will undoubtedly lead to mutual respect, in the long run.

MANAGING IN-LAWS

Dear Lady A: I've always had a tricky relationship with my in-laws. How can I work on getting them to like me more?

I believe the answer to your quandary lies in your question. You are under the impression that you need to conquer the mountain alone. Indeed, what will make this impediment much easier to surmount is having your beloved partner by your side to assist you. These are their parents, are they not? Therefore your partner should offer the support you need and stand in your corner, advocating for your charm and wit, and all of the excellent qualities that serve as evidence for why they chose you in the first place.

The more one tries to make people like them, the harder it can become to secure their good opinion. You should not overextend yourself to win their approval, especially if they have made no attempt to curry your favor. But that does not mean you should not aim for kindness whenever you are in their company, for kindness can be as effective a weapon as a rapier. Behaving in this manner will only have the benefit of disarming them. Who can ever withstand the power of a compassionate word?

SUPPORTING FAMILY IN DIFFICULT TIMES

Dear Lady A: My family has been dealing with a big loss. What can I do to be there for them without neglecting myself?

My utmost condolences to you and yours in your time of mourning. In my day, there was a widely understood period in which society expected us to mourn—namely by donning black clothing, and foregoing all social invitations for possibly up to a year and a day, depending—but quite honestly, everyone grieves in their own fashion. Make sure you treat your family—and yourself—with kindness. Mourning can't be rushed, and while time does heal wounds, it may not lessen the sting of memory.

Understand the ways in which you can lend support to your family while taking care not to neglect yourself. Perhaps they would appreciate being relieved of a chore they dislike. You could offer to replenish their cupboards? Most importantly, make time to share fond memories of the past with one another, which can make the burden of grief feel a bit easier to bear. By and by, your despondency will not be so overwhelming, but until then, permit yourself and your loved ones understanding in the process.

CREATING A FOUND FAMILY

Dear Lady A: I've been estranged from my biological family for a while, but I've managed to fill the void with people who care about and support me. Is a found family still valid?

My dear, the most marvellous thing about families is that no two in existence bear a single resemblance to one another. The point of family is not its composition, or who exists within it—but the fact that it exists. Any family can really be defined as a coterie of love and contentment in seeing all of its members succeed and thrive in life. It does not matter whether this group of kin happens to look like any other you may know; what is paramount is that you are bolstered by people who only have reason to lift you up rather than diminish your light. Similarly, they are the ones who receive your affection and reinforcement in return.

The family that you have created for yourself through trial and experience is just as important and full of meaning because of what it provides to you in your greatest times of need. Regardless of its construction, or the ways in which its members may or may not be related to one another, its existence is what matters.

It makes this lady's mood glow with happiness to think of you surrounded by those who will provide you with the greatest support—especially when you may not have been so cared for in the past.

Treasure them deeply, and take steps to remind them of how important they are in your life whenever possible. A family tree successfully thrives when all of its branches are flourishing to their fullest potential.

CHAPTER FOUR
ETIQUETTE & APPEARANCE

First impressions, careful reader, are crucial.
They can mean the difference between an instantly
charmed companion and someone whose good opinion
is forever lost. It is key to put your best foot forward
in every interaction—with said foot clad in
the best slipper or boot available.

It is not merely the external that should serve
in winning over others; manners are equally
beneficial to master. From perfecting the
aesthetic of your abode to knowing which
items are a must-have in your reticule,
let me be your guide in how to
be proper, both inside
and out.

PERFORMING RANDOM ACTS OF KINDNESS

Dear Lady A: It feels like there's so much negativity in the world. How can I perform more good deeds for the people around me?

Firstly, it is someone of noble spirit indeed who possesses the intention to bring more good to everyone around them. But intentions only do so much good without actions to further their reach. In that vein, you can certainly make your corner of the globe that much brighter.

If you possess a skill in baking, try making a batch of cookies and calling on your next-door neighbor for company and conversation. When you are out running errands, consider paying for the person who is next in line behind you.

For those of you who may live in a remote corner of the country, there are still means you can take to spread some cheer and good will. Send messages to loved ones that you may have lost touch with in recent months, purchase them a small gift that isn't attached to a special occasion, or even a simple message to show they are on your mind. Often, all we need to improve our day is the knowledge that someone out there is fondly thinking of us.

PROJECTING CONFIDENCE

Dear Lady A: How do I work up the nerve to order from the cute barista at my neighborhood coffee shop? Sometimes I'm so tongue-tied that I forget my own name! Help!

Firstly, it is quite beyond me why anyone would elect to imbibe coffee when it is quite well-known that tea is the fashionable drink of choice in society these days. (Of course, there are certainly ways of improving the taste of coffee; this writer opts for a bit of sugar and a splash of milk.) But, I suppose, if you must insist on your large mocha something-or-other with extra whipped cream and sprinkles (how decadent!), here are a few techniques that will allow you to project confidence while adhering to the highest level of etiquette for this particular situation.

You may have heard the saying, "fake it till you make it". Namely, if you act outwardly confident, confidence will follow. Ensure that you loudly and plainly state your name, and be sure to clearly enunciate — I cannot think of anything more embarrassing than being addressed by the wrong moniker when claiming your order. Remember: it may even be written on the side of the cup that you are permitted to take away with you, so take pains to ensure that it is very obviously *your* portable beverage. You wouldn't want someone else to mistakenly snatch it up for themselves—and after all, the attractive barista is far more likely to remember your name if you state it clearly.

Ultimately, it never hurts to err on the side of politeness, either—like accepting your tall decaffeinated cappuccino with a smile and a word of thanks. You might even be able to strike up an idle conversation with this charming crafter of coffee, at least, provided the line behind you has not grown too long.

PERFECTING THE VIBE OF YOUR LIVING QUARTERS

Dear Lady A: I just moved into my first apartment, and I get to decorate it all myself! How do I find the perfect look for my living space?

You want your living quarters to be a place that will warmly encompass you when you return at the end of a long afternoon, breathing a sigh of relief as you cast off your outer garments and don a banyan or dressing gown. Even writing it now makes this lady long for the hour when it is socially acceptable for her to retire for the evening.

The answer to your enquiry is that there is no right answer, because what one person might prefer in terms of overall colour scheme or furniture options may not be the same as another's personal tastes. Indulge in many decorative throw pillows. Display your favorite art throughout. Splash a bold color of paint on the walls. You can certainly replace it with another if you decide you don't enjoy it after all. Your home is your space and can be a lovely reflection of all your favorite things, however weird and wonderful. This author gives you unfettered permission to be as experimental and daring as you like!

TABLE MANNERS

Dear Lady A: No matter what I do, I can't seem to avoid spilling food on myself whenever I'm enjoying a meal. How do I keep my clothes looking perfect?

S o many meals seem to have been designed with the sole purpose of making them as difficult as possible to consume. Just think of the sheer quantity of soups that are served at any given dinner party!

From the very beginning of our time in society, we ladies are taught how to consume from a bowl without slurping, as well as the proper way to grasp a spoon so we do not embarrass ourselves in front of others. This all takes a significant amount of practice, so do not fret if you do not immediately master it. Like all skills, it takes patience and effort to finesse.

One way to safeguard your impressive wardrobe is to drape a napkin over yourself. Tucking it into the collar should be avoided at all costs; you do not want to appear as if you are wearing a bib as part of your outfit. After you have ensured that your lap is successfully covered, use another rather simple trick: tilt yourself ever so slightly forward over your plate so that any spare drops of soup or sauce will fall onto it and not you. The last thing you might try is to simply wear all black so that if you should happen to drip onto your clothing, it will be much more difficult to spot the stain, affording you time to return home and scrub it away. If anyone asks why you are clad in dark colours, you may tell a small fib that you are in your period of mourning. What they do not know certainly will not hurt them. Problem solved!

TURNING DOWN
AN INVITE

Dear Lady A: Last week, I turned down an invitation to hang out with a friend and then felt regret afterward. How can I feel positive about staying home?

How can you be expected to win over everyone you meet if you are wilting as a result of overtaxing yourself? Not to mention that dark circles under the eyes are a highly unwelcome addition to anyone's appearance.

Therefore, this lady recommends that you give yourself permission every once in a while to turn down invitations. In addition to affording you some much-needed time for self-care, sending your regrets every once in a while has the added bonus of giving you an air of mystique!

With that in mind, try serving your own needs with small indulgences at home. First and foremost, give yourself a true night of relaxation, whether that involves drawing yourself a hot bath, picking up a good book, enjoying a glass of strong claret—or even all three at once. Dispense with looking at your mobile device, or set it to "do not disturb" while you let your mind rest. It may be tempting to check in on what your friends are pursuing during their separate evening excursions, but this will only exacerbate your feelings of missing out.

Second, try to ensure that you arrange a future date by which to see your compatriots again; having something to look forward to in the future will assist with any anxieties you may be experiencing in the present. You will be able to return to your friends as the best version of yourself—they may even inquire about your secret to looking so resplendent!

HOSTING A DINNER PARTY

Dear Lady A: Recently, I moved into a new apartment and I want to invite a group of friends over for dinner. How can I throw the best party?

~~~~~

There are few skills as valuable in this world as knowing how to throw a fabulous soirée. Reputations within the *ton* can be made or broken solely based on whether one's event is successful. Many still speak fondly of the Duchess of Dorsetshire's summer fete and her marvellous 10-course meal, which included blancmange, pickled grapes, hashed calf's head, and lamprey eel—and that was five years ago!

Settle on a theme if you wish, but otherwise, you can choose a desired color scheme for your table arrangement as well as your place settings. Flowers make an attractive centrepiece, though this lady has heard talk of an exotic fruit called the pineapple that has come into fashion—you can even rent them yourself! It may also behove you to settle on a menu ahead of time, whether you are preparing the dishes yourself or purchasing the services of a chef to assist you. While it may be tempting to serve one large meal for everyone to partake of, dividing your dinner into several courses will make the entire event feel that much more elegant. Handwritten cards placed before every seat will ensure the most ideal opportunity for engagement among your guests—for example, you would not want to place two wallflowers next to each other if you wanted to encourage conversation! After the meal, most parties would see men and women divided from one another, but rather than cigars and claret, keep your guests together for the pursuit of games and amusing trivia questions. You will send them home with stomachs filled and minds stimulated at the culmination of an enjoyable night.

GETTING A PET

Dear Lady A: I've been thinking about getting my first pet. When do you think is the right time to welcome a four-legged friend into my life?

When it comes to animals intended for companionship, one pet is very much in fashion amidst the *ton*, though this author is convinced that too many ladies consider their little yippy lapdogs more of an accessory than a creature whose welfare should be upheld. But therein lies the advice you seek, which is that opening your home to a domesticated feline, canine, equine, or something else altogether should happen when you are best equipped to personally take care of them.

A dog or a cat (or great heavens, even a lizard) can be a darling friend and a wonderful balm to cure any feelings of loneliness; who among us would not enjoy being greeted the very moment we enter our home? But having a pet is also a practice in reciprocity, for you must equally tend to their needs and ensure that they are content. Start by providing a setting in which they canflourish and thrive. One cannot take adequate care of a horse in an apartment, for instance!

HOW TO
SURVIVE A BALL

Dear Lady A: My friends have been trying to get me to go to the local club for weeks. How can I put my best foot forward on the dance floor?

Dancing is certainly a way to make a good impression on others, whether you are participating in a waltz, a quadrille, or what this writer understands is the more commonly wielded form of movement... merely gyrating one's body about. How scandalous! And to think, there is not even so much as a dance card for a lady to keep track of who has asked her to partner in a cotillion! While the usual rule would demand that any unattached woman wait for a gentleman to extend an invitation to take to the floor, such a requirement no longer exists. Therefore, you are entirely within your rights to reach for a dear friend of any social standing and proceed to move as the pace of the song encourages, whether a slow ballad or a faster jig.

I must also remind you of the importance of consistent refreshment. One understands these exhilarating dances can be taxing on the body, and that the establishments in question can become quite crowded and overly warm, leading to severe flushes. Do not forget to take breaks every so often, especially whilst partaking in a glass of punch or lemonade. If there is a terrace on which you might take in some fresh air, so much the better. It would not behove you to become lightheaded—or, worse yet, so overcome that you find yourself swooning, especially away from a divan, which would make it possible to do so more becomingly. Of course, keeping your dearest bosom friends within close reach will also enable them to observe those times when you are in dire need of respite, and vice versa. All the better to spare your feet as well, which will inevitably ache after a lively and unforgettable night out!

THE IMPORTANCE OF THE RIGHT ACCESSORY

Dear Lady A: I've bought a new outfit to wear to work, but I can't decide which accessory to pair it with. When it comes to that side of fashion, I get stuck!

My dearest friend the Viscountess of Waverly once took me aside at a summer soirée and, as politely as she could, said, "Darling, sometimes less is more." At first, I was distressed by her assessment, but then I came to realize that in this particular instance, she was absolutely right. In my desire to pair several different accessories to my new dress—including fan, reticule, several strands of pearls, matching earrings, and a rather large headdress—I looked more like an overstuffed peacock than the most fashionable lady of the *ton*. *Quelle horreur!*

So, if I can dispense any advice upon you now, it is this: learn from my tragic misstep, and do not fall prey to the temptation to wear every piece of jewellery in your possession, for you may be at risk of blinding your fellow partygoers instead of making a fabulous entrance into the room. When in doubt, subtract one, or perhaps even two, accessories if necessary. Minimalism is key.

HANDBAG ESSENTIALS

Dear Lady A: What are the must-have items I should keep close at hand for every occasion?

The most important thing that any lady can have on her person is a reticule—compact but capable of storing small items of worth. A fan, to not only stave off the heat of warm days but also to signal interest in a potential dance partner. Gloves, since to go without can be seen as rather gauche. A shawl or a hat is also invaluable (sunburns are very unbecoming). There is also a new invention of tinted glasses, which can help you avoid the act of squinting.

Other modern inventions may be stowed in a satchel—such as a single reader on which hundreds of books can be stored at once! Shillings should also be tucked away in a pouch made for that express purpose. You might also carry a tube of cosmetic lip colour to revive your complexion. If you require items to freshen yourself up, you could carry a pack of chewable gum, or a small bottle containing a liquid that sanitizes the hands—two things every member of the *ton* could have made use of, in my day!

DISCOVERING YOUR PERSONAL STYLE

*Dear Lady A: My friends seem to know their own
personal style inside out, but I'm not happy with most of what's
in my closet. How do I find the best fashion version of myself?*

I will let you in on a lesser-known secret, advice-seeker:
there is nothing more stylish in this world than having
the utmost confidence in whatever you are wearing.

The first step in reaching that, however, must be a willingness
to experiment—maybe even outside of your initial comfort
zone, especially if you feel less than inspired by your
current trousseau.

In other words, you must be prepared to be bold and take
chances, because in many instances this can result in a
marvellous pay-off. However, you don't necessarily need to
make every change at once. One way in which you can spruce
up your existing look is by adjusting your coiffure, or even
dyeing it a different shade altogether. Incorporate different
accent pieces into your current wardrobe, like a new pelisse
or wrap. Gradually and over time, you will discover the most
fashionable version of yourself.

CHAPTER FIVE
WORK

Alas, where there is play and fun, work inevitably
follows. While hours of toiling will always be less
desirable than more entertaining pursuits, employment
is unfortunately a necessity for the modern individual.
But that does not mean you should not find ways to
enjoy your time doing so—however and wherever
your wages are earned!

Whether you are attempting to discover an
occupation tailored to your interests, or seeking
some leisure time for your own health,
continue reading to learn how you can
balance your hard work with just as
much marvellous leisure.

PROCRASTINATING

Dear Lady A: I have a huge project due at work the day after tomorrow, but I keep getting distracted. How do I force myself to stop procrastinating?

Dearest reader, how many of us have been trapped in a situation where we would rather be doing anything else—and then while away hours in a day doing everything but the task we were supposed to be completing? But this tactic of avoidance will create only more difficulties for you later, as well as more turmoil when you realize you have even less time to acheive your goals than you thought.

The trick therein is not to overwhelm yourself at the very end by leaving things to the last possible minute. With this project due sooner, structure out your remaining hours by dividing it up into smaller portions to accomplish. Each milestone reached can include a specific break or reward.

It may be slow-going, but it will benefit you more in the long run if you've got something to look forward to at the end of each task. This technique has benefitted me during many an afternoon filled with necessary chores, and hopefully it will work to your advantage as well.

WORKING OUT WHAT TO DO WITH YOUR LIFE

Dear Lady A: I've just finished studying and am having trouble pinpointing where I want to start looking in terms of jobs. How do I find the career that's right for me?

E mbarking on any significant change in life can be an intimidating prospect! When we ladies concluded our (admittedly limited) schooling and had a choice between the pursuit of starting our own families or tutoring the children of another, it could leave one nearly paralysed by indecision! Ah, but I see you are actually speaking of occupations—which are a noble pursuit, to be sure. These days, there are a significant number of possibilities for everyone, which is likely the cause of some of your indecision at the moment. Why, if what I have heard about modern society is to be believed, anyone can work as a physician, or an author, or even hold a position in government if they wish to!

Should you continue to experience indecision, this author would recommend that you make a simple list of each potential job's positives and negatives. Seeing the advantages as well as the drawbacks may make it easier to narrow down your options. If you still cannot make up your mind after that, know this: you do not have to be locked into one occupation for all of eternity. It is quite possible for you to change your mind whenever you wish to! You might decide to work at a modiste and then find that your heart leads you to daringly pen a scandal sheet under an alias instead. You are the best advocate for what will make you the most content in work and in life, but that can also look differently depending on where you are in said life. The ladies of my day may have been required to fit a certain mold, but you, my dear, are perfectly equipped to break every one of them.

WORKING FROM HOME

Dear Lady A: I'm working from home and struggling to turn off my brain at the end of the day. How do I establish a clear divide between work and relaxation?

A s this lady understands it, in this day and age working duties in the home apparently do not include accepting invitations to tea and other social engagements. However, you can employ some tips and tricks in order to make your particular situation more tenable, especially if you work in the same place where you shed your slippers, put up your feet, and relax at the end of the day.

You must delineate a place for yourself to work that is separate and unique from your bedchamber. Toiling hard in the same room where you rest your head will only make it more difficult for you to differentiate between work and recreation. If you are able, make use of a small writing desk or your sofa rather than your bed.

Most importantly, at the end of every day, cease responding to correspondence. No electronic letter is so important that it cannot wait until a new day begins.

ESTABLISHING A MORNING ROUTINE

Dear Lady A: When I commute into work, I have trouble leaving on time. How do I motivate myself to get out the door in the morning?

In times like these, the author is certainly sympathetic to your plight—and to think, you are responsible for taking the reins, metaphorically speaking, and transporting yourself, without even so much as a footman to boot! But one of the easiest methods to inspire motivation, particularly if you are not inclined to rise with the sun in the morning, is to go to bed early so that you may ensure you get a proper night's sleep. (Few things are as unbecoming as dark circles underneath the eyes!) This will ensure that it becomes less difficult for you to drag yourself from your bed and perform your ablutions, especially if you lack a lady's maid or valet to assist you with getting dressed.

Taking the time to break your fast is also imperative, even if you can bring yourself to partake in only a small nibble. Something is better than nothing, and you must fortify yourself for the long day ahead, at least until you can break for luncheon.

This lady also understands that these days one does not take a hansom cab from one destination to another; rather, one drives an automobile or perhaps even takes the railway train or motorbus. So many options to choose from, but of course, traveling the same route back and forth can grow tiresome. Why not bring along a book to read or listen to in order to make the trip more bearable? Reserve the story for your shuttling only and then you will be desperate to fly out the front door so that you may learn what happens next in the torrid romance between Miss Penelope Prendergast and the dashing Duke of Devonshire—or whatever tale strikes your current fancy. Happy commuting!

REQUESTING A PROMOTION

Dear Lady A: I've been at my job now for a few years, but I think I'm ready to take on more responsibilities. How do I approach my boss for a promotion?

The person who is the best arbiter of your strengths and what you are capable of achieving is yourself. If you feel you have reached the threshold of your performance in your current role—or even find yourself somewhat underwhelmed by your present duties—then this lady sees absolutely nothing wrong with advocating for a grander position with even more authority. In cases like this, try writing out all of the achievements you have already reached, as well as the reasons for why you deserve the promotion that you are seeking. Having a list to glance over can also suffuse you with the confidence you need to approach your employer, especially when your strengths are fresh in your mind.

Once the meeting is secured, plead your case. You will recall that list I asked you to make? Use those as the points around which to build your argument, plainly explaining how you have put in the effort and hours to merit you this furtherance. An approach of self-assurance in yourself and what you have to offer will undoubtedly impress your superior.

QUTTING YOUR JOB

Dear Lady A: I've been growing more and more dissatisfied with my job recently. How do I know when it's the right time for me to quit?

Your question actually reminds me of a personal tale from my own life. We ladies of the *ton* are frequently encouraged to pursue a vocation intended for our own betterment. However, yours truly struggled through many of these activities. My fingers are not intended to wield needle and thread, they are too clumsy to attempt anything musical on the pianoforte, and they cannot render even so much as an apple's likeness! It took time and patience—perhaps a certain level of impatience as well—before I realized my temperament was best suited to putting pen to paper.

The larger point I make here is that you should not toil away in a position that makes you anything other than most content. When should you take your leave, you ask? Right this very moment! You can decide to arrange an alternative form of employment to offer peace of mind before taking the plunge, but when it comes to your immediate future, the time to seize happiness is now. You are far more likely to regret the chances you did not take than the ones you did.

IMPRESSING AT AN INTERVIEW

Dear Lady A: I have an interview coming up for a job I really want. How do I wow them enough to ensure an offer comes my way?

It is understandable to face nerves ahead of something that requires poise and the best outward-facing version of yourself—but you can take steps to bolster your resolve! Do not spend the night before fretting: get rest. Your mind should be clear as you prepare for your interview—which leads to the next part of my advice: dress for success. This is how you can make an impression before you so much as open your mouth to speak. Freshly laundered clothing, with any hems mended, will serve best.

Be sure that you have adequately researched your prospective employer on the off-chance they enquire about your knowledge of them. However, they will likely pose most of their questions about you, and this is where you can be the most prepared—who knows you better than yourself, after all? Take as much time as you need to answer what is asked, and conclude it all with a proper thanks. What follows is the wait to be contacted—but hopefully, with good news!

FACING A BAD BOSS

Dear Lady A: My boss has always been pretty unbearable, but recently their behavior has become impossible to ignore. How do I deal with all this stress induced by a bad manager?

This sounds quite troublesome, and I'm certain that being confronted with such an emotionally taxing situation day in, day out is only harming your productivity levels! As loath as I am to concede any ground to difficult people in general, especially those who seem to derive personal enjoyment from making others miserable, I would hate to see you continue to languish in an environment that will bring you only worry and strife.

You do not owe this supervisor your effort and energy, and I doubt you can perform to the best of your ability under these conditions. You certainly don't deserve to dread your arrival at work each morning, or to count the hours until you can flee out the door. If you can, try reaching out to your HR department whose job it is to help in situations like these. If that remedy doesn't improve things, begin looking for a new position that brings you joy and fulfilment.

Dear Lady A: My coworkers usually go out for happy hour drinks every week. They've been asking me to join them, but I'm nervous to let loose around them. What do you suggest?

Firstly, this is a positive sign of camaraderie. Consider yourself officially ingratiated with your colleagues if they have extended an invitation for you to join them in their weekly venture to the tavern. While you may feel some apprehension about striking a balance between friendly and professional behaviour, there is benefit in getting to know your peers without the stresses of your profession looming overhead—and doing so responsibly, even in a more relaxed setting!

You can try your hand at a round of darts, or see how you fare at billiards. Apparently, one newer game that you could attempt revolves around two teams throwing balls into cups from across a table—although you will be required to drink the contents afterwards, which this lady finds incredibly unseemly. Keep track of what you imbibe, and be sure to marry your liquor with alternating glasses of water; you would not want to be in a poor state at the office the day after!

AVOIDING BURNOUT

Dear Lady A: Lately, I've been working a lot of long hours, and it's starting to stress me out big time. How do I avoid becoming seriously burned-out by my job?

M y darling reader, while there is certainly time for work and committing yourself to the occupation of your choosing, it is also imperative that you seize advantage of leisure opportunities whenever and wherever possible. Why, just look at the *ton* on the whole. Anyone who is anyone makes a point to retreat to the country or the seaside every summer when the weather becomes unbearably warm. It also takes one away from the hustle and bustle of the city to a world that operates at a much more relaxed pace. Certainly a welcome change, I must tell you, and and all of us are forgiven for wanting a respite from society's watchful eyes and wagging tongues. (In fact, I dare say that a fine majority even prefer to live as freely as they can, far from the gossips who would readily speak on anyone else's business but their own.)

You should take a leaf from those who settle into a more sedate pattern while taking their summer sojourn — and do not shy away from treating yourself to the vacation you wholeheartedly deserve. If you have a weekend to spare, venture down to the beach and dare to remove your shoes and stockings to feel the cool saltwater on your toes.

Better yet, if you can afford a longer trip, make preparations for that jaunt across Europe that you have always longed to pursue but continually discouraged yourself from taking. You'll return rested and refreshed, with a rather bold tan by extension, and will have made many thrilling memories that you can turn into equally exhilarating anecdotes to impress your colleagues. *Bon voyage*!

TAKING A CAREER BREAK TO TRAVEL

Dear Lady A: Recently, I've been thinking about quitting my job and taking a break to travel abroad like I've always dreamed. How should I free myself to follow my dreams?

This author will have to live vicariously through you, aspiring wanderer, and the prospect of this nomadic existence. I can picture you now, walking along the open trail with a pack of necessities strapped to your back and your face tilted up towards the sun!

To transform your dream into a reality, ensure you have finances well in hand. You would not want to become stranded with no money for your return passage, so set aside funds for this trip as well as any potential emergencies. Look into taking alternative work during your travels, so you will have a small source of income. You can either plan with excruciating attention to detail or choose a place on the globe at random and see where your journey takes you. You should also take care to write home so that friends or family can track your whereabouts. Chronicling your travels will also allow you to fondly reflect on the memories you make.

CHAPTER SIX
BE YOUR BEST YOU

We come to the conclusion of this invaluable
tome! While all of the previous chapters are
certainly filled with my salient guidance, this one
holds the most vital yet: how to reach the best
possible version of yourself.

The secret to achieving this is not to focus on what
others are doing: no two roads to contentment will
run the same. While I do dispense important and
very sage advice, perhaps the best advice of all is
not to cling too closely to others' words.
Only you truly know yourself and can
forge your own path, and you must
not be afraid to go your
own way.

GIVING BACK TO YOUR COMMUNITY

Dear Lady A: I've been looking for ways to offer my time to good causes outside of work or hobbies. Do you have any suggestions for how I can give back to my community?

Many members of the *ton* believe that the wealthiest individuals are the ones most worth befriending—but it is this lady's firmest belief that it is what one chooses to do with said wealth or time that makes them truly rich indeed.

There are always charities that could use a kind donor to assist with sponsoring their greatest needs. But money is not the only means through which to assist others. You can also lend your time through volunteer work, by packing boxes of food and toys, for instance. If you have clothes in your wardrobe that you no longer have need of—such as a spare parasol, day gown, bonnet, or pair of gloves—consider freeing up the space by donating them to those who would benefit from them most. Whether you are the next heir to an impressive title or one who strives to make their own way in the world without plentiful offers to their name, you can still give of yourself. You already have a generous spirit and a keen instinct to use it well; your community will benefit from your thoughtful efforts in whatever form they take!

ASSERTING HEALTHY BOUNDARIES

Dear Lady A: I often have trouble making time for myself in my busy schedule. How can I learn to put my own needs first?

The first recommendation I would give is to seek patience with yourself in this process. Growing forthrightness is not an overnight act, especially when it comes to establishing boundaries between work and leisure time. In fact, it will take some time to build up your inner fortitude, so do not fret if you struggle to find your most assertive voice. Most ladies of the *ton* are encouraged to keep their thoughts to themselves; any greater expression of opinion is considered gauche, but the alternative is enabling someone to operate without consideration of your physical and mental limits!

Think of your well-being like a muscle—the more you work it and exercise it, the stronger it will become. It is equally important to prioritize your own needs even when you are feeling your most refreshed, rather than waiting for catastrophe to strike before taking action. When necessary, call on a trusted friend or family member to bolster your efforts if you need someone to hold you accountable in remembering to take time for yourself. Beginning with smaller changes before working your way up to defining greater limits can also help. Refrain from answering missives from work during hours that should be spent in relaxation — perhaps breathing in the fresh air or cooking a nice meal, or calming the mind with meditation. Putting yourself first and foremost in everyday needs will better equip you to do the same in larger life decisions — whether in your relationships or your career path.

CUTTING DOWN SCREENTIME

Dear Lady A: I'll admit I have a problem: I am glued to my phone, but I don't know how to change that. How can I break my screen addiction habits?

I see you are writing of the dreaded handheld method of communication, which has eclipsed many other forms of entertainment thanks to its portability and capability to contain a great number of avenues for personal amusement. (I believe you refer to them as *applications*.) Nevertheless, this author is struck by the disadvantage of focusing all of one's attention on something in the hand. Think of what you might miss out on if you are so intent on chirping out every thought that crosses your mind.

The best solution to your struggle is to replace the hours you spend gazing at a screen with other pursuits. Put on your boots and go walking on the moors for a spell if the weather is favorable. Pick up the book you have been meaning to begin time and time again. Call on a friend at their home and catch up on all the latest society goings-on. Eventually, you will realize that nearly an entire day has passed without you needing to look at a screen at all.

STANDING UP FOR YOUR BELIEFS

Dear Lady A: Sometimes I have trouble voicing my opinions, especially when I'm talking to more assertive people. How do I find the courage to speak my own truth?

There are those in this world who will tell you that a woman who speaks her mind is improper. But in truth, standing up for one's beliefs does not merely involve being forthright in conversation with those with whom you are already familiar. It also includes self-educating on those causes that you are passionate about—and a willingness to take action on behalf of rights that you are more than entitled to! You may find that you are predisposed to composing a letter to those who represent you in the political sphere or to donating to a local campaign, rather than taking to the streets for a local march on rights and reform, but any method of engaging with a movement that represents something important to you is powerful in its own way.

Those you might worry yourself over, the ones who would criticize you for taking initiative when it comes to your beliefs, are not worth lending a second thought. While it is important to hear both sides of a discussion, you would be better off surrounding yourself with individuals who respect and validate your opinions—even if there are times when you may politely disagree! It can be rather isolating when you feel as though you are the only one who holds a particular belief, especially if you are often confronted with naysayers who attempt to dominate any debate in which you participate. In those instances, seek out groups of people who feel as you do, so that they can uplift you in your perspective and even become new friends. The next time you must face a very prejudiced person, you will be equipped with all you require to confidently address them with your head held high.

STICKING TO YOUR RESOLUTIONS

Dear Lady A: Every new year, I try to set a resolution for myself, but I always have trouble keeping it. How can I stick to my personal goals?

A new year is always full of new possibilities, especially when it comes to the act of bettering oneself! But it can be rather difficult to maintain momentum, even after you have established a promising start for yourself, for any number of reasons.

What this lady would suggest instead is creating smaller milestones that can be surmounted much more easily first. If you have never attempted an afternoon jog, take a light one through the village instead of signing yourself up for a grueling marathon. If you are trying to learn the harp, familarize yourself with a single piece before you offer to perform at a salon. You can devise little rewards for when you reach these small goals on the way to your larger resolution. Treat yourself to a new novel or that striking accessory you have been coveting in your favorite shop's display. Move forward with sights set on your immediate achievement rather than your ultimate destination.

FEELING LONELY

*Dear Lady A: I struggle with
loneliness on a regular basis. What can
I do to combat these feelings?*

While this author can think of several instances in
which solitude is one of the most desired states you
can achieve—a peaceful walk in an open field with bonnet
clasped in hand, or taking paint and canvas to sit at a nearby
pond and render the view—what makes these moments
noteworthy is having sociability to oppose them. When
blissful solitude crosses over into loneliness—and a persistent
one at that—that is not a happy condition in the slightest.

What I will tell you now is that everyone, no matter who
they are, at least once in their life has combatted these very
feelings. It can seem very isolating to be lonely, until you
realize that loneliness is a state shared by many of us.

However, in the moment, this can be difficult to perceive,
especially when you have already convinced yourself that you
are the only one in the world who has ever experienced
loneliness. The fortunate news is that you can take steps to

fight against these feelings, and they begin and end with seeking pursuits that remove the temptation to wallow in your thoughts and instead propel you into some form of escape. Call on a friend and invite them to accompany you to the bookshop or the nearest coffee house. Go walking in the closest park, or have a picnic beneath the inviting shade of a large tree. The more isolated we render ourselves, the lonelier we become, so give yourself permission to venture out into the world!

RESISTING COMPARISON

*Dear Lady A: I struggle not to weigh my
accomplishments against my friends'. How can
I learn to be satisfied with my successes?*

There is a saying that perfectly describes your position,
and it goes something like this: the harvest always appears
to be more fruitful on the other side of the fence. I believe
whoever coined that proverb was speaking from personal
experience, because the conundrum you find yourself in is
one of the most universal. We are, all of us, so often in
want of that which someone else has, but this is because
we mistakenly presume that what we do possess is somehow
lacking or inferior by comparison.

Would you believe me if I told you that those very friends
whose achievements against which you feel compelled to
measure your own have likely envied your success on
occasion? You should, not only because I have an impeccable
sense for these things, but also because it is also true.

Now, conquering that instinct—the one that says one is not
as worthy because one has not accomplished the same number

of things that others have — is not a war that can be fought and won overnight. If it was, that little green-eyed goblin we know as jealousy would not exist! What ultimately assists in combatting this tendency, however, is celebrating the smaller victories rather than weighing the value of purported greater triumphs. Be proud of what you have done, even today, and what you will do tomorrow, and the day after that. And as for the particulars, *que sera, sera*. You make an impact solely by existing, and this world is all the better for it.

FEELING HAPPY IN YOUR OWN SKIN

*Dear Lady A: I've always
had a big self-confidence issue. How do
I learn to love the skin I'm in?*

While it is widely believed that others are most inclined to criticize us, you might be shocked to learn that this is a false assumption. There are none who are more fault-finding in that regard than ourselves. We are incredibly prone to looking at our own reflection in the mirror and cataloging every single supposed flaw we might encounter. We may think that the rest of the world is aware of these so-called imperfections, but the truth is that we are the ones most likely to notice the areas in which we believe we are lacking.

This lady believes that everyone is in possession of traits that are unique to them. All that is required is you becoming aware of their loveliness. The next time you happen to glance in a looking-glass, track the attributes that satisfy you instead of focusing on the things you dislike. (This part can be easier said than done, but I assure you it is possible with some practice.) Then, take steps to flatter or highlight them whenever possible! Try on a bold new lip paint that accentuates the shape of your mouth, or don a handsome suit jacket that complements the broad set of your shoulders. You have qualities that no one else in this world possesses, and they are worthy of pride and a bit of gentle bragging (but not too much). Emphasizing your best features will also likely result in you receiving the compliments from others that you deserve, especially if you exude confidence and poise in yourself! Overall, it is important to take care of the aspects that make up your form, and the more attention and love you give them, the better you will feel on the inside as well as on the out.

INDEX

ACKNOWLEDGEMENTS

They say it takes a village to raise a child, but the same can be said for a book. I am indebted to the team at DK Books—chief among them my editor Flo Ward and my copyeditor Claire Rogers, who helped shape this book into the best version of itself. *A Regency Guide to Modern Life* would not be nearly as whimsical were it not for the incredible talents of Jo Podmore. This book is as much your triumph as it is mine! I also want to thank my family and friends, for cheering me on through every deadline, and my dear pal Preeti Chhibber, for graciously answering every single writing-related question I sent her way. Lastly, this book would not have existed, period, without my husband and bonafide romance hero, Spencer, whose belief in me gave me the courage I needed in myself.

AUTHOR CARLY LANE is a journalist who specializes in covering the entertainment industry with a particular focus on film and television, as well as her first and foremost love: romance novels. Her writing has appeared in various publications such as *Vulture, Collider, Paste Magazine, the Boston Globe, Vice, Teen Vogue, SYFY Wire*, and elsewhere on the internet.

She lives in Atlanta with her husband, aka her own real-life romance hero, who obligingly builds her the occasional extra bookshelf in an attempt to combat her eternal tower of TBR. You can find her on Twitter @carlylane, where she spends most of her time there talking about her favorite reads and spreading the good word of romance to anyone who will listen.

ILLUSTRATOR JO PODMORE is a UK based digital illustrator with a background in traditional mediums. She has a passion for colour and loves to create narrative illustrations in a playful and often humorous, contemporary style. She has also illustrated for greetings cards, stationery and children's books.

You will frequently find her at the theatre or in a gallery. But most often, lost in a book. You can find her on Instagram @joey_pod and at www.jopodmore.com.